Love, Marriag & Growth

A poem anthology

Shemique Blair

Life is a journey not a destination.
- Unknown

SHEMIQUE BLAIR PUBLISHING CO.

MOOSE FACTORY, ON

Love, Marriage, Divorce & Growth
Copyright © 2020 by **Shemique Blair**

All rights reserved. No part of this publication may be reproduced, distributed, or transmitted in any form or by any means, without prior written permission.

Shemique Blair/Shemique Blair Publishing Co.
P.0. Box 626
Moose Factory, Ontario P0L 1W0
www.sblairwritings.com

Publisher's Note: This is a work of fiction. Names, characters, places, and incidents are a product of the author's imagination. Locales and public names are sometimes used for atmospheric purposes. Any resemblance to actual people, living or dead, or to businesses, companies, events, institutions, or locales is completely coincidental.

Book Layout © 2017 BookDesignTemplates.com
Book Cover Design © 2020 ebooklaunch.com

Love, Marriage, Divorce & Growth/ Shemique Blair. -- 1st ed.
ISBN 978-1-7772933-0-7

Tellwell Talent
www.tellwell.ca

ISBN
978-0-2288-4138-8 (Paperback)
978-0-2288-4139-5 (eBook)

Dedicated to my family and friends, with all my love.

I am grateful to have been loved and to be loved now and to be able to love, because that liberates.

–MAYA ANGELOU

Foreword

Thank you for joining me on this journey of my experiences of love, marriage, divorce, and growth. Poetry has been around for thousands of years and poems are written to share ideas, convey emotion and create imagery. This anthology is an expression of emotions and an intentional shift in mindset that has taken place in my own life during the different phases I have encountered. I hope that these poems inspire you, amuse you, and cause some reflection during whichever place you find yourself in your own life.

Contents

SECTION I LOVE 1
Crush 2
First Date Quirks 3
Stirrings of first love 4
Mine 5
Precipice 6
What is love? 7
SECTION II MARRIAGE 8
How beautiful 9
Our commitment 10
Intimacy 11
Together 12
Mad 13
I'm sorry 14
Love steady 15
SECTION III DIVORCE 16
The demand 17
Misery 18
Heartbroken 20
Over 21
Skeletons 22
SECTION IV GROWTH 24
Forgiveness 25
Letting Go 26
Single Again 27
Dating 28

Take me back to those days	29
A new connection	30
Live a life	31
Finding Me	32
Growing pains	33

SECTION I LOVE

At the touch of love, everyone becomes a poet.
- Plato

Crush

I've got a crush on you.
Butterflies,
Sparks fly,
At the twinkle in your eye.

My cheeks flush,
My palms sweat,
And a sappy smile spreads.

Will he ask me?
Is he interested?
Who should make the first move?!

Anticipation
Crackles the air
Breathe held as we stare...

Would you like to go out sometime?
— I'd absolutely love to!

First Date Quirks

I

Went on a ride to the breezy river
It was so cold, I got the shivers,
Got my bum back in the car
He hit the seat warm
And said, "Heating up my snack for later!"

II

His hair bang had me in envy,
It was long, shiny, and wavy
I gushed with glee:
"You like a bang, I see!"
In astonishment, he gaped at me...

Stirrings of first love

The unexpected,
Giddiness that energizes my limbs
Is a persistent distraction
From the completion of mundane tasks,
What is this feeling?

Reckless desire
I have never encountered
Yet so familiar.
Has stolen my focus and
Snared my thoughts.

Have we met before?
Has karma surfaced, to rejoin past souls?
To where will this lead? I wonder.
Is this what I *think* it is?

My questions overwhelm in
An attempt to make sense
Of the effervescent cascade of emotions
Shattering and reshaping my world.

In wonder, I am stunned,
Blindsided by love.

Mine

Gently you take your hand in mine,
    Our fingers entwine like grape vines.
My breath halts as a shock jolts,
    Up my arm.

Striking my heart in a staccato thrum,
    Thrown from my comfort zone,
I paused.

In the next moment my axis righted
    And everything made sense...
Looking into your fathomless eyes, I knew.

The hunter had met the hunted,
    You. Were. Mine

Precipice

I stand at the precipice.
Seeing how vulnerable you have made me,
When did this happen?
When did I let my guards down and let you in?

I stand at the precipice seeing
The power you have to undo me,
Unravel me,
Shred me in deep love and passion.

I am an open book —
Eagerly, craving your penmanship.
Your stroke awakens my soul.

I stand at the precipice
A willing captive to your thoughts and desires
Matching an echo deep within me.
Under your perusal I blush, I blossom.
You
Tantalize
Me.

And as I look out, into the horizon,
I realize with certainty:

I
Want
More.

What is love?

Love is selfless,
    In its effort to please others and nurture.
It acts in grace.

Love is compassionate.
    With forgiveness and understanding,
Extended across time and space.

Love is accepting.
    It belittles not,
It is an open canvas ready to be embrace.

Love is gracious.
    Thoughtfully exchanging the gift of intimacy—
With humility in place.

SECTION II MARRIAGE

And over all these virtues put on love, which binds them together in perfect unity.
- Colossians 3:14

How beautiful

How beautiful it is when two souls embrace,
A perfect fit, a match made.
A heavenly gift,
Like a rainbow after rain.

How beautiful it is when two souls dance,
Soft like snowflakes in the palm of my hand.
In your eyes I see a millennium of futures...Ours.
Unbound, our love flies higher and higher

How beautiful it is when two souls overcome,
Like a child's first step into the unknown.
Uncertainties cannot stifle love grown,
But only fortifies lovers to saunter on.

How beautiful it is when two souls blend,
In a union as deep as still waters.
'My love, with this ring, I thee wed,
To have and to hold, forever and ever...'

Our commitment

When I think of you, I melt.
Warmth spreads throughout.
United,
Our commitment leaves no doubt.

Our life together makes me proud.
A wife to you,
A mother to be—
Your safe place in times of need.

You are a husband whose care and love shines.
We'll be friends always, lovers throughout time.
It is an honour
To claim you — as you have done I.

Through the good times, the bad times
And in between.
We extend love, respect, and trust to each.

Intimacy

What is Intimacy?
More than the physical.
It's the time you take to offer a compliment
And the priority you show me.

It's the late-night phone calls
Just to 'check in',
And words of appreciation
Of things that don't go unnoticed.

It's the warmth of your smile
And your intense gaze into mine.
That stretches a moment of silence
Into a lifetime of shared memories.

It's the comfort of knowing
You're my safe place—
My deep breath of peace,
When the doors close and the world recedes.

Together

I succumb to the need to nurture,
And hold you close in the protection of my arms.
This is how I express my care toward you.

I am your shoulder to lean on
I am your stalwart support.
The weight of difficult decisions
Is a load we bear, but never alone.

Hand in hand,
We take it all on,
And fiercely conquer,
The atlas of our dreams and goals.

Together, we are fearless.
Together, we overcome.

Mad

You make me so mad; I could curse like a sailor!
I explain and explain but you adamantly disagree.
In that impervious tone you say,
"Hun, it's not meant to be."

It's like I'm explaining emotions
To an artificial being.
My feelings matter but you only crave logic.
Maybe you'd find it— if you removed that stick...

We argue in circles over the same *damn* thing!
You said and I said...I said but *You* said,
Voices never raised but sharp tones intended
To drive home the conclusion.

The occasional snort of derision
Grating on nerves gone thin
I huff and walk away in annoyance, shouting:
"You're sleeping on the couch tonight!"
"Like hell I am!", You respond in kind.

I'm sorry

I'm sorry.
I hate when we argue.
It's not that important in the long term,
And honestly, I miss you.

Can we compromise?
I said some things I didn't mean.
I sincerely apologize
for hurting your feelings.

It's okay that we don't agree
But let's be united in one thing:
I love you
And you love me.

I'm not always right,
And neither are you.
But let's be open
To the other's point of view.

Love is the fragile exchange of trust
And the hope of much more.
I desire to share my heart and my life with you.
Please trust me with yours.

Love steady

Love steady when seasons change,
And uncertainty reigns.
True Love will calm fears,
And conquer pain.

Love steady in times of grief
And turmoil,
For the times are telling of greater things
Than you and I.

Love steady and cherish your loved ones,
Today, hold them close.
For many will sup from that plate of slumber
'When?' We will never know.

Love steady and treasure those memories,
Lest they fade.
For every moment spent is a lost opportunity
Time flies— wake by wake.

Life is unpredictable,
Life is fragile
Love steady despite!

The days are short, and the nights are long,
Some have broken, already left, and passed on.
...Love steady while the day breaks,
And may the heavens smile as love reigns.

SECTION III DIVORCE

A divorce is like an amputation, you survive but there's less of you.
- Margaret Atwood

The demand

Side by side,
I affectionately greet you
With a smile.

Moving in to embrace,
I see a change
In your physical space.

Leaning back,
My gaze encounters
Your dull eyes.

Removing my arms,
Shifting backwards,
I wait.

Your hands loosely
Lay on your thighs,
As you exhale on a relieved sigh.

"I want a divorce."
You demand,
Decisively.

Misery

I hurt with a pain so deep-
My soul laments in agony.
Your words, "I want a divorce."
Left no time to adjust to the anguish.

Swift and ruthless,
Your request lacerated
My heart.

The gravity of your demand,
Pummels like angry fists beating against flesh.
My body immobilized by shock and grief.
My mind uncomprehending,
The magnitude of the moment.

My safe ground shifts,
Like quicksand beneath my feet.
Shattering,
My emotional cocoon,
My sense of stability.

I watch them disappear,
Like a once vibrant landscape,
In the wake of a volcanic ash cloud.

Inconsolable, I struggle to,
Pick up the pieces of my fractured heart,
Collating the last vestiges of my dignity.

Depression blankets my soul
As loneliness follows.
Oh, such misery!

Heartbroken

Do you know how *hard* it is?
Not to reach out and touch,
Hug or embrace you?

We have become so distant.
I do not know how to act around you.
Emotionally displaced,
I stay out of your way, avoiding you...

You have made it perfectly clear
That you do not desire me.

Our conversations are stilted,
Vague,
And without substance.

Things I would openly share
I now keep close.
Proceeding with caution.

Our brief contacts are uncertain,
Stiff and cold.
If separation from me is what you truly need,
Then I can do no more,

Than to acquiescence
To your wishes,
I am heartbroken.

Over

We've lost the attraction.
We've grown apart,
And want different things.

Seven years
Of tears,
One broken commitment.

Conversations with my girlfriends,
"Have you tried counselling?"

Prayers,
For reconciliation.
Pitiful hopes of understanding
Led to the end of our beginning,
Where the only choice was acceptance.

It is over.
Ink has dried on our divorce papers.
Forebodingly, premonition whispers,
"The grass is never greener…"

Skeletons

We all have skeletons that remind us,
We all have skeletons that haunt us,

When I take the time to take stock of my life,
I can find myself mourning old friendships,
Too superficial to hold any substance worth lasting...

Memories of laughter fade under the hurt and confusion,
Loyalty turning to betrayal and bitterness,
Left wounds too deep to mend,
You were my friend.
Or were you ever?

We all have struggles,
But you took suffrage in your chains,
And chose to humiliate others to cover your insecurities,

Refusing to acknowledge your faults and mistakes,
Instead, seeking to place blame on my shoulders...
Misplaced burdens led me to shake free,
And resurrecting dead relationships has lost its appeal...

We all have skeletons that remind us,
We all have skeletons that haunt us,

Yet when I take the time to take stock of my life,
I sometimes find myself mourning old friendships,
Which I now realize,
Were never worth lasting...

SECTION IV GROWTH

There is no growth without discontent.
- Unknown

Forgiveness

It took a long time, I admit.
I'll be honest
When I said the words, "I forgive you."
That was only the beginning.

I still had to grieve.

And that thorn dug deep,
Through layers of thick skin,
Embedding into my circuit—
A' trip- wire' that paralyzed me.

For months I moved in a haze
In blind disbelief.
A strained smile on my face
As I encountered each new day.

I said those words and meant those words:
"I forgive you."
Because Love is self-less.
"I forgive you."
—In order to heal me.

Letting Go

I let go
To allow room
For new growth.

In Spring,
Under an exuberant sun,
Leaves bloom on
Fertile deciduous trees,
After a stark,
Winter's cold caress.

Like those same leaves,
My heart blossoms
To a new season.

Single Again

Single again...*yay?*
At the age of thirty,
What a depressing thought...
It's hard to see the optimistic ray.

The nights are so lonely,
I dread the coming end to each day.
Going home to an empty space.

Quiet evenings,
No welcome greeting,
This is my new escape.

I miss the laughter, teasing
And silly games,
The home cooked meals,
Thoughtful discussions,
And witty debates...

Now a grim silence,
Echoes in its place.
Getting used to my own solitude
While old memories replay.

Dating

Dating is a game to some,
A facade of simpering,
Gleaming intent,
Often promising no more than,
A temporary satisfaction.

Dating is a puzzle to others,
An intricate web of design,
Meant to capture unknowing prey
Into a fool's paradise.

Dating is a second chance for a few,
Hoping to recapture a youthful dream,
To wipe a tarnished slate clean
And begin anew.

Take me back to those days

Take me back to those days, simpler days,
When time stood still in my childish gaze,
When superheroes were real and,
My dreams were already made.

Take me back to those days...
When friendships were pure,
No thoughts of deceit,
Only innocence,
And playing 'hopscotch' in the streets.

Take me back to those days...
When the sun rays kissed soft upon my skin,
Felt like momma's warm embrace,
And hearing the ice cream truck,
Brought a grin to my face.

Oh, take me back to those days, simpler days
When true love was a principle,
And the goodness of humanity was untouched.
When hopes soared,
And heaven was a goal,
That meant somethin' to us...

Oh, take me back to those days...

A new connection

Thoughts of you conjure a smile,
A shiver,
A sigh.

A new connection...
A pleasantly teasing sensation,
That tickles my interest,
My mind and emotions.

I anticipate and thirst for more
Fill me, with more...
Of your wit, your humor,
Your authenticity.

I could devour you—
Completely.
Utterly entrench you within,
The depths of my folds.

Will you allow me close?
Grant me permission,
To sink within your barricade.

And settle beneath...
Is there room enough for me?
May I nestle deep within your heart
To find,
A haven for mine?

Live a life

I want to live a life that inspires,
Another to dream and take risks,
Against obstacles of doubt and insecurity.

I want to live a life that has purpose,
And meaning—
Where every step I take,
Leaves an imprint.

I want to live a life that is so pleasing,
Death would sigh with jealous ambition,
And envy the living.

I want to live a life that inspires,
Future generations to climb higher.
A life that pleases my parents,
To be proud of their daughter.

Finding Me

After letting go,
I am free to wonder—to dream.

After letting go,
I am free to choose a different option for me.

After letting go,
I can expand my capacity into new ventures,
Take risks and accept a challenge.
I can bend, I can twist,
I can pivot.

After letting go,
Finding the me,
I never allowed to be,
Is now a possibility.

I run, I fall, I scrape a knee,
Pick myself back up, brush off,
And keep on going.

Turning the page,
Onto a new leaf...
Finding me,
I can see, will be a life-time journey.

Growing pains

Transitions are difficult,
Trying to stay balanced while,
Sand shifts under my feet.
Life lesson learned:
Plans are never concrete.

Growth stretches endurance,
And ways of thinking.
Molding one's character,
Through painful life lessons.

Change is scary,
It's the ultimate risk.
Sacrifice is often required,
But is so worth it.

I will never know,
If I don't begin.
Make me a student— willing to learn...
Again, and again and again and again.

About the Author

Shemique Blair is an educator, writer, dreamer and singing enthusiast. She lives in the northern regions of Ontario, Canada, with her indulgent cat, working to make a difference in the lives of those she encounters. She is an avid reader who still believes in true love and romance.

Printed in Great Britain
by Amazon